Acknowledgements

Acknowledgements are due to the following authors, from whose works short extracts have been quoted purely to illustrate the acting career and performance achievements of Orson Welles.

William Blake, Samuel Coleridge, F. Scott Fitzgerald, Graham Greene, Ben Jonson, Herman Mankiewicz, Herman Melville, Friedrich Neitzsche, William Shakespeare, Orson Welles and H. G. Wells.

Edinburgh Fringe Festival 2004
Souvenir Edition Limited to 500 copies

WORLD PREMIERE

ROSEBUD - The Lives of Orson Welles

Author
Mark Jenkins

[signature]

Director
Josh Richards

[signature]

Actor
Christian McKay

[signature]

Festival Souvenir Edition Number

84 / 500

Published by infestedwaters.co.uk

First published in Great Britain in 2004

Mark Jenkins is hereby identified
as the author of this work in accordance with
section 77 of the copyright, designs
and patents act 1998

ISBN 0-9543842-6-1

Published by   infestedwaters.co.uk
                      Ty Ganol, Rhodiad y Brenin
                      Saint Davids, Wales

In association with Discover Press, 103 Henderson Row
                      Edinburgh EH3 5BB

Design and digital production by Jane Messore

Printed and bound in Great Britain by Automedia Limited

ROSEBUD
The Lives of Orson Welles

by
Mark Jenkins

The set is empty and fully lit. House music is Anton Karas playing 'Café Mozart'. Centre stage is a table and chair. A hat-stand, rear left, bears cloak and other props. As the show is about to start, the stage darkens to blackout as the music fades out. From the darkness, a window filter, high right, immediately beams down on Welles, wearing a Trilby, his face half-shadowed by the light, with an enigmatic smile and a raise of the eyebrow as in 'The Third Man'. At this point, the music changes to Anton Karas playing 'The Harry Lime Theme' from The Third Man. Welles holds this pose for a few seconds. A 'coup de theatre'. The light fades to blackout…A shot rings out and kills the music. Snap spot.

WELLES*: 'That was the shot that killed Harry Lime. He died in a sewer beneath Vienna. Yes, that was the end of Harry Lime. But it was not the beginning. Harry Lime had many lives, and I can recount all of them. How do I know? It's very simple… because my name is Harry Lime…'*

Cut!

On the cue 'my name is Harry Lime'- general wash. Welles walks forward, tosses Trilby on to table. The Harry Lime theme starts up again, as he meticulously lights up a cigar.

WELLES
(Shouts to sound/lighting technician) O.K. That'll do for the opening shot. Lou ! Could you turn the damn music off, please? *(Music stops)* Thank you! *(He enjoys the cigar and scrutinises it, still bantering with the technician)* There isn't a restaurant in the world I can walk into without Anton Karas and his goddam zither dogging my every footsteps! That was nineteen forty-nine. Anyone would think I'd done nothing since!

(Still talking to technician) O.K! Let's run it through, from the top! (HE STEPS FORWARD ONE MORE PACE AND GOES INTO PERFORMANCE)

(To audience)
Good evening, Ladies and Gentlemen, my name is Orson Welles.
(He blows out a cloud of smoke and places the cigar down in an ashtray on the table)
Or is it?… Can we ever be really sure in this business?… This artifice. This fakery. It's often hard to know where reality ends and subterfuge begins. Why! Tonight I could be just a figment of someone's perverse imagination! That's the magic of it. What's that, Sir? 'Am I a charlatan?' Well, Sir…I'm still working on it!

You know, I still go to parties in the hope that I'll get asked
to do the tricks I mastered as a kid. I was at Louis B. Mayer's birthday –
the boss of M.G.M -
I guess I get invited as a punishment. I'm sitting at a table
with my top hat, cloak and cane – secreted in my trouser leg,
a small white bunny rabbit. Who should grace the stage but Danny Kaye,
doing a routine that just goes on and on. The rabbit is as good as gold.
Then Judy Garland sings…and sings
(she could go on singing till the cows come home).
The rabbit starts to nibble at my underwear. As dawn comes up
somewhere over the rainbow at the Hillcrest country club,
… pellets are appearing at my feet,
Al Jolson's singing 'Mammy!' and the rabbit is peeing all over me.
Groucho Marx advises me to change cologne and asks:

'Say, Orson, what's the secret of a magic trick?'

'It's how to get the rabbit out of your pants!'

(He advances, arms outstretched)

'But pardon, gentles all,
the flat unraised spirits that have dared
on this unworthy scaffold to bring forth
so great a person; can this cockpit hold
the vasty fields of… Welles? Or may we cram
within this wooden O the very casques
that did affright the air at …Hollywood?
Now entertain conjecture for a while!
On your… imaginary forces… work.'

Prologue

From the time I am barely able to breathe, everyone I know
is telling me that everything I do is wonderful.
And not just wonderful, but unmatched in the annals of babyhood.
'My! Doesn't he take the breast well!'
'Look, look! Walking already! What a mover! You're the greatest!'
'What! Reading books at only three! You're gonna make Professor, honey!'
Fresh out of diapers and I'm scraping tunes on the violin. I'm told –
'Even Mozart couldn't play that well, this age!'
And when I start piano, it's *'Eat your heart out, Paderewski!'*
Every day, a miracle! My childhood verses put Dante to shame.
Houdini bows his head to my simple magic party-tricks.
School plays? My mother sends a message to the world.
'Watch out John Barrymore! There's a new kid on the block!'

Have you any idea what all this adulation does to an impressionable child?
He begins to believe it, that's what! He expects success in everything he does.
And in expecting it, he's half-way to achieving it.
He becomes insufferably confident, an indefatigable achiever –·
quite simply a pain-in-the-ass Jack-of-all-prodigies!
Like that little bird, the cuckoo, he grows too big for the nest,
shouldering out all the other little chicks, so he gets all the goodies.

Of course, I'm no damn good at football. Athletics leaves me cold
and I yawn profusely at baseball games.
And since I'm never going to make it to the army,
I guess that five-star-general is on hold.
In any case I doubt that they'd have need
for an overweight, flat-footed, exhibitionist with a bad back
and a tendency to question every order from on high.
Congressman perhaps? Or Senator? President is more my style.
It's just a roller-coaster, road-show after all! All smoke and mirrors.
No, I can't rule out the dismal art of 'politics'.

Small Town Boy

Small-town boy at sweet sixteen
(pronounced a genius at only eighteen months)
with rosebud lips and only half a nose. Conceived in Rio;
born half-way from Milwaukee to Chicago and heading for the milky way
of stardom. Sixteen and barely shaving, yet – actor, writer, keen director,
showman and producer; sound-recordist, lighting man and choreographer!
School-kid-maestro, impish impresario – struck by lightning morning, noon and
night!
Fresh out of 'The Shadow', shorts and candy –
innocent of the evil that lurks in the minds of men;
motherless child with a father who follows, on cue, soon after;
demonic cherub with a booming baritone
(it kind of threw them, coming from the baby face!)
Sword-swallower, painter, puppeteer and pianist;
Chinese explorer, magic trickster, female impersonator.
Tall boy with a short list of three guardians to play the role of 'Daddy'.
(I choose the Jewish one – well, he *was* my mother's lover – did I have a choice?)
I've already played a rabbit with a slick line in sales talk;
The Emperor of Rome, no less; Androcles *and* the Lion (in the same show!);
Doctor Faustus, Doctor Jekyll *and* his sidekick, Mister Hyde.
Busting out of school at night to ravish Woodstock girls –
well I can't neglect my sexual education –
You don't get *that* at Todd school for boys, unless you're so inclined.

So what's it to be, George Orson Welles? 'George' will have to go for starters.
My father figured every Pullman porter in the country was called 'George'.
Nobody gets anywhere much with a name like 'George',
or, if they do, it's by default. But 'Orson' is awesome and 'Welles' will do nicely.
Wells – enchanted hollows, shrouded round with ferns, haunting, dark; –
havens of the saints with healing waters for the sick,
drawing strength and magic from the centre of the earth;
where pilgrims come to render homage from afar.
Yes… wells. That's me – Awesome Welles!

Poor Dad! Well, rich Dad, actually – not the 'stinking' kind, but comfortably wealthy.
It would be ennobling to regale you with stories of extreme adversity,
of poverty and angst and serial homelessness,
but God, in his waywardness, denies me these advantages.
I have to fight my way from mid-western affluence
to the destitute state that is my destiny.
Why! I don't even know where my next glass of sherry is coming from!
But Dad did – it came from the drinks cabinet, with all the other drinks.
He made a fortune from car-lamps –
invented them about the time cars needed lamps. He was pretty damn smart
and drank himself to death as a form of self-congratulation.
Ended up some place called 'Grand Detour, Illinois'.
'Grand Detour' – is that a metaphor for something?
I used to visit there – a hotel of faded glory. Dad owned it.
The place was full of girls with painted toenails
and no visible means of support,
lolling around on Chesterfields.
There were jugglers, acrobats, illusionists – drop-outs from the world of vaudeville.
I guess the old inventor saw something of himself in them,
inventors are magicians after all!
Rub a car-lamp and out will pop the genie – money!
"Mysterious gold! Embracing close, impossibilities!"

Not that my mother couldn't have made her own way, rather well, had she so
chosen. Suffragette and champion crack shot with a rifle, but most of all –
a concert pianist for whom the arts were held in reverence.
She admired the 'sophistication' and 'complexity' of dear, old Europe –
an affordable indulgence thanks to Dad and Henry Ford.
She probably never thought to ask herself why long lines of
sophisticated, complex Europeans were besieging Ellis Island!
Yes there's a lot to be said for Grand Detour, Illinois!
The illusionists are harmless, the jugglers don't wear jackboots
and the tricksters don't do the goose-step!
Anyway Mom dies too soon to realise where all this European sophistication
is heading and no-one can blame her for that.

Am I my mother's or my father's son?
I suppose we all ask that with parents now and then.
(Time's blood-coil winds it's way to us, through them),
and I can answer truthfully, as we all can when we're thinking straight –
both of them. Art is manufacture and manufacture, art.
We make them both and make them happen.
Yes, if you want to work magic with movies,
you have to conjure up the money first!
And that's the toughest trick in the book!

Father Figures

I only get to appreciate Dad's gift to me much later,
when it's too late for me to make amends.
I mean, just think about it! There am I, my father's favourite son, –
calling my mother's lover, Maurice Bernstein, 'Dadda' to his face
and he returning the affection with my pet name …'Pookles'!
It gets worse. I adopt a *third* father, Skipper Hill,
my doting headmaster back at Woodstock.
Skipper and Dadda insist I give
an ultimatum to my own flesh and blood.

*'Quit drinking or I can't see you anymore.
You're a bad influence on me.'*

And this from an ungrateful brat, who has every advantage
lavished on him! …My brother Richard is, frankly, cast aside
to languish in a mental institution all his life…
He's the unseen victim in all this…
When I think of what my father did for me –
he gave up business so we could discover the world
together, just me and him! – Is it any wonder
he drank himself to death? What would *you* do?
He also must have known, as he lay dying,
that my inheritance would be slowly eaten away.
This was Hamlet, Lear and Falstaff all rolled into one.

I think it was Nietzsche posed the question:

"Can you bring yourself to will the eternal recurrence
of everything in your life, down to the last detail?"

Only those who answer 'yes' can inherit his Godless universe.
I think of that each time I play Falstaff, rejected by Prince Hal.
We, all of us, play both roles at different times in life.
I guess I played the Prince too young
and I've been Falstaff ever since.

Life is a wonderful introduction to Shakespeare.
It all happens there first. I get the bug early
and never quite manage to shake it off.
I appoint my own headmaster as my first assistant director
and start adapting Shakespeare as a full-time occupation;
not as an esoteric study of 'Elizabethan drama',
but a manual for living; making sense of here and now!
And when I leave school, I do Shakespeare 'live' on radio,
using an ambulance to speed me through the traffic from
one studio to the next. (You see, I have to do 'soaps'
to pay for my addiction to the classics.)

I make it my duty to deliver the Bard to his rightful owners –
plain, ordinary folk, who don't know what a 'folio' is and
regard him as a bald and bearded English bore,
whose plays are stuffed full of quotations!

Mercury

In all honesty, the state of theatre is hardly uppermost
in other peoples' minds. There's a bigger drama
playing in the streets of all our towns and cities.
Millions stand in line for soup and hand-outs,
while millions more can't even spare a dime for charity.
Then Franklin Roosevelt, in his wisdom, decides
to get the jobless back to work – and that includes
the artists, writers, actors and directors.
Roosevelt knows man does not live by bread alone.
His generosity is gratefully received by all.

And just to prove that nobody, but nobody is excluded,
John Houseman and I stage Macbeth – in Harlem with an all-black cast!
Our vehicle for achieving this is the Federal Theatre Project.
Instead of witches – voodoo witch-doctors, beating out Haitian drums!
An atmosphere of elemental tropic storms,
with wind machines, unleashes black Macbeth's unbending
lust for power. And Banquo's killers do the deed with guns.
It's an everyday story of Harlem gangs.
I tell you, the opening night is like a football game.
The cops have to rope off four blocks around Seventh Avenue.
Harlem folk are fighting for fifty-cent tickets.
It's the blackest first night in American theatre history.
It runs ten weeks and tours all over!
Don't anybody ever tell me Shakespeare's 'inaccessible'!
You just have to let his magic speak.
A white Macbeth meant nothing to them,
but Black Macbeth is being lived out every day before their eyes.

The reviews we get are all superlatives –
except for one …by Percy Hammond of the Herald Tribune.
A member of the cast called Abdul approaches me
to ask permission for a voodoo curse to silence him.
It sounds like a lot of fun, so I agree, and the drums begin to beat.
….Next day, the guy's in hospital… and he's dead within forty-eight hours…
Have we any critics here tonight? Check out your life insurance!

According to our articles of association,
we are supposed to be 'politically neutral'.
That's kinda tricky with a guy like Marc Blitzstein on board.
He writes a musical called 'The Cradle Will Rock!',
about a ruthless steel baron who runs a place called 'Steeltown'.
It's dynamite, because, just as we launch,
the steelmen and the auto-workers decide to strike
and things are getting pretty violent on the labour front!
The government regards the play as 'dangerous'
and puts armed guards around our theatre
on West Forty-first Street…So, I march the entire cast
and audience twenty-one blocks up Broadway
to do the show and make our point. Tell you what…
if I had to do it all again, I would. We did right.

It's like some elemental force has swung behind us.
For now, it happens. We proclaim the launch of 'Mercury'.
Our 'Declaration of Principles' pledges classics at low prices
and that's exactly what we give them. It starts with…'Caesar'.
Maybe we should have called it 'Brutus'
because it's more about the noble-minded liberal,
confronted by the onset of an age of tyranny,
dictatorship and ruthless, regimented power.
What is a liberal to do? How should he react?
In 1937, millions of Americans were asking just that question.

(Performance piece. Blue filter)

'...But 'tis a common proof
That lowliness is young ambition's ladder
Whereto the climber upward turns his face;
But when he once attains the utmost round
He then unto the ladder turns his back,
Looks in the clouds, scorning the base degrees
By which he did ascend. So Caesar may.
Then, lest he may, prevent. And since the quarrel
Will bear no colour for the thing he is,
Fashion it thus: that what he is, augmented,
Would run to these and these extremities.
And therefore think him as a serpent's egg
Which hatched, would, as his kind, grow mischievous,
And kill him in the shell.'

But the irony is this – though I play the part of Brutus,
in my directorial role I am transformed into something like a Caesar.
I'm only twenty-two and all the critics say that theatre
has undergone a revolution. But in the process, so have I.
Show after show we are packing them in to witness Mercury in the ascendant
- until our loyalties to Blitzstein's friends are scabbily repaid.
Yes, 'Danton's Death' was done to death by those for whom the story
was too close to home. A tale about a revolution that goes sour
and then degenerates into a reign of terror. We're talking 1938.
We're in the middle of rehearsals when we're confronted with
a delegation…from the American Communist Party…

'You do realise the interpretation that might be put upon this play?'
' We realise that it's of great contemporary relevance, yes.'
'And do you propose to put it out in its present form?'

'Well, we're not about to make changes that might compromise the drama.'
'So, effectively, you are quite prepared to play into the hands of the enemies of the revolution? Is that what you're saying?'
' We make the artistic decisions here.'
'...With funding from the Federal government?'
' Don't try to blackmail us. It won't work.'
'Perhaps we should remind you, we have people working on this show who might pull out.
What's more, we bus in more than half your audience, every night. It would be a pity to lose them.'

We have the rug pulled from under us.
They sink the show. We don't get audiences.
Finally, the government winds up the Federal Theatre Project
and we are crushed from left and right.
You just can't fight a war on two fronts.
But I still have magic up my sleeve!
I think its time that drama on the radio
was confronted. The Mercury revolution has only just begun!

War of the Worlds

For me to get excited with a script, I have to feel I'm walking
on a fraying tightrope, twenty stories up, above a busy six-lane highway.
It helps if there's a stiff breeze and no safety net, with bookies laying
ten-to-one against, I'll never make it. Then, I'm interested.
My Mercury Theatre On The Air is doing fine enough with classics,
but, let's face it, 'Jane Eyre' is never going to get listeners rushed
into emergency with heart-seizures. John Housemann, my producer, recommends
we dust off a nineteenth century sci-fi novel and
I decide to set it, not in sleepy England's yesteryear,
but in the here and now - as a live newscast in New York City,
where, it turns out, there are more hyperactive neurotics
than we bargained for. Their nerves are, no doubt, jangled by Hitler's
ranting and his strutting hordes in that distant planet, Europe.
It's a quiet Sunday in October,1938, on the eve of Halloween.
From the start, We make it very clear that this is a drama and open with these
words…

(Radio Performance. A CBS mike is taken from the wings. Spot. Welles' tones are theatrical, as in the recording.)

WELLES AS ANNOUNCER: The Columbia Broadcasting System and its affiliated stations present the Mercury Theatre on the Air with their adaptation of The War of the Worlds by H.G.Wells….

(Mercury Theatre Musical Theme; Tchaikovsky Piano Concerto No.1)

WELLES AS ANNOUNCER: 'Ladies and gentlemen, the director of the Mercury Theatre and star of these broadcasts, Orson Welles…

WELLES: *We know now that in the early years of the twentieth century, this world was being watched closely by intelligences greater than man's and yet as mortal as his own. We know now that as human beings busied themselves about their various concerns,*
they were scrutinised and studied, perhaps almost as narrowly as a man with a microscope might scrutinise the transient creatures that swarm and multiply in a drop of water… Yet across an immense ethereal gulf, minds that are to our minds, as ours are to the beasts of the jungles; intellects: vast, cool and unsympathetic, regarded this earth with envious eyes and slowly and surely drew their plans against us.

In the thirty-ninth year of the twentieth century came the great disillusionment. It was near the end of October. Business was better. The war scare was over. More men were back at work. Sales were picking up. On this particular evening, October thirtieth, the Crosby Service estimated that 32 million people were listening in on radios…"

(He leaves the mike momentarily)

Then we give a casual weather bulletin for that very day,
a short news-wrap, some soothing music from Ramon Raquello and his orchestra. And just as some might be reaching to switch stations…

(returns to mike, using different 'newsy' voice)

" Ladies and Gentlemen. Following on the dramatic developments announced
earlier tonight, we interrupt this programme to go live to our reporter,
Carl Phillips, at the International Observatory at Princeton, New Jersey, for
the latest observations of the planet Mars, from world-renowned astronomer,
Professor Carl Pierson"

(Welles plays Professor Pierson. Calm and sceptical)
" Nothing unusual at the moment, Mr Phillips... A red disc swimming in a blue
sea. Transverse stripes across the disc...Quite distinct now, because Mars
happens to be at the point nearest the earth. They're not canals, I can assure
you Mr. Phillips,
although that's the popular conjecture of those who **(amused)** imagine
Mars to be inhabited. From a scientific viewpoint, the stripes are
merely the result of atmospheric conditions, peculiar to the planet.
I should say the chances of there being ...**(chuckle)**...little green men on Mars
are about a thousand to one. And if there were, the distance between us and
them, forty million miles, is a pretty safe one.
(Ominous change of tone)

But as for those massive eruptions you reported earlier....I have to say
...I simply can't account for them..."

By this time, new listeners, have tuned in. And they have no idea
that all they're listening to is a Halloween hoax.
Next they hear the newscast being interrupted again
to go 'live' to our supposed Martian landing sites.
One reporter gets zapped by death rays in mid sentence.
Then it begins. The real drama.

**(SFX begins in distance building up so that soon Welles is having to
raise his voice. Blue flashing lights. Police sirens. Bells ringing. Sounds of
pandemonium, to background music of Holst's 'Mars' from 'The Planets')**

These poor deluded folk are jumping into cars
and heading for the hills. Traffic lights are out of business.
There's panic in the streets. Churches are filling up with congregations they
never knew they had, while priests are turning atheist.
There's tearing off of garments, great wailing and a gnashing of teeth!
The shelves of grocery stores are stripped.
The cops arrive in the studio but don't know who it is they should arrest.
(SFX begins to fade, slowly)
All over the east coast, switchboards are lighting up like Christmas trees
in police headquarters, hospitals and government offices!
So, half way through the show, we put out a reminder:
'Hey! This is just a play!' By now, it makes no difference.
(SFX ends)
And if the press is to be believed,
I am facing lawsuits of around twelve million dollars!
The next day, at the press conference, there wasn't
a CBS executive to be found anywhere….
They were all in hiding! There was…just, me!

*(Flashlights of cameramen at a noisy (SFX) press conference. Welles is seated,
looking young, harassed, defensive, apologetic and concerned)*

*' Were you aware, Mister Welles, of just what terror was going on out there in
the streets? Our listeners want to know!*
Why no! Absolutely not! When we did 'Dracula' it didn't have that effect. When
you're doing a radio show, you have no idea of who's listening or how many…It's
just you and the microphone…Perhaps nobody at all is listening…
Honestly, it was a complete surprise to us.
'And how do you feel about it now'?
Why! We're just as shocked as anyone…

*(End of Press conference. Fade. Welles stands. The defensiveness has now
vanished. He's pretty pleased with his surprising coup)*

People tried it in other countries and were put in jail.
I was sent to Hollywood.
So now I have a reputation to live up to.
Three years later, I'm doing a broadcast for the government, when I'm interrupted
by the newsflash that Pearl Harbour has been bombed.
The President actually calls to ask me to put out a statement that it's for real.

Kane

And so, the Martian has landed!
My namesake, H.G.Wells has done me proud.
Time to lay waste Hollywood…and the studio system.
Watch out boys! Flee to the hills!
The bug-eyed monster's a-comin to getcha!

(Welles steps forward as Prospero. He proclaims)

'………………………………………*I have bedimmed*
The noontide sun, called forth the mutinous winds,
And 'twixt the green sea and the azured vault
Set roaring war; to the dread-rattling thunder
Have I given fire, and rifted Jove's stout oak
With his own bolt: the strong-based promontory
Have I made shake, and by the spurs plucked up
The pine and cedar; graves at my command
Have waked their sleepers, ope-d, and let 'em forth
By my so potent art.'

Enter left, George Schaefer of RKO pictures.
'Mr. Welles. We're offering you a contract.
What say you write the screenplay and star
in 'War of the Worlds'? We're talking big, big money.'

'It's not the money', I reply, *'I want authority.'*
Four pictures of my own choosing!
Act, write, produce and direct!'

Schaefer thinks I'm crazy, but he gets more ardent with each rejection,
until, finally…*'O.K., you maverick son of a bitch. You got it!'*

Four movies. It's unprecedented. It's also universally resented!
They have ways of dealing with magicians in L.A.
I am pronounced 'a homosexual'
by 'Big Boy' Williams in a cowboy bar,
as he cuts my tie off, at the knot.
We settle it with fisticuffs, outside, in the car lot.

(Pensively)
Imagine you are barely twenty-four and the Wizard of Oz has given you
the biggest electric train-set the world has ever seen…and a playroom
the size of a movie studio for a party lasting two whole years.
You can invite all your friends, stay up late and no interfering parents are allowed.
I'm wild again! A mischievous child again!
Little Orson Annie with a licence to kill, amaze
and generally outrage the elders of the tribe of Babylon!
I am the first free man in Planet Hollywood.
And all the studio galley-slaves are willing me to screw up, big time.
I'll never have another chance like this!

(Practically)
Where to start? Why, at the end of course. Start at the end and work backwards!
Herb Mankiewicz and I are going to pick a fight with the biggest bully
in the playground and kill the bastard off in the opening reel.
Then we can party at an autopsy of movie-length. We'll call him 'Kane'
(well Abel's not around to tell the tale). Soon every playground bully
in the heart of darkness is protesting that the movie's about *him*!
All of them are right, of course, but chief amongst them, William Randolph
Hearst,the man who did for newspapers what Stalin did for camping holidays
in Siberia.

Five people tell their stories of the Kane they knew.
Five different and conflicting stories, the sum of which do not add up to one.
'He was some kind of a man. What does it matter what you say about people?'
Isn't that how life is for all of us?
Your friend, your enemy, your lover, wife, or son
will see the you *they* knew.
Yet something's always missing when your race is run.
We call it… 'Rosebud'…

(Performance piece – newsreel journalist, Rawlston. Exaggerated expressionist lighting. Shadow on the walls. Rawlston wanders thoughtfully, occasionally snapping out orders to unseen waiting reporters) BLUE FILTER.

*" When Mister Charles Foster Kane died, he said just one word…Rosebud… Yes Rosebud. Just that one word – but who was she? Here's a man who could have been President, who was as loved and hated and as talked about as any man in our time – but when he comes to die, he's got something on his mind called 'Rosebud'…Now what does that mean? Find out about Rosebud! Get in touch with everybody that ever knew him. That manager of his (**snaps fingers**) …Bernstein… His second wife – she's still living! See 'em all! Get in touch with everybody that ever worked for him, who ever loved him, who ever hated his guts!…I don't mean go through the city directory of course! Rosebud, dead or alive! It'll probably turn out to be a very simple thing…"*

And yet, you can't help but like the young usurper
–Charles Foster Kane. He's brash. He's confident.
It is the confidence of a truly profound ignorance.
Kane's in the office of his new crusading newspaper – The Inquirer - when his guardian and fellow shareholder drops by to counsel caution.
He wants to stop the Kane campaign against big business!

(Exaggerated expressionist lighting. Large shadow on the wall. The youthful Kane is tilted back on his chair, arms behind his head. As the scene progresses he briskly circumnavigates the table addressing an imaginary Thatcher. Kane begins light heartedly) BLUE FILTER

"I was expelled from college – a lot of colleges – you remember? I remember. Mr Thatcher, the trouble is - you don't realise you're talking to two people. As Charles Foster Kane, who owns eighty two thousand, three hundred and sixty four shares of Public Transit, Preferred – you see, I do have a general idea of my holdings – I sympathise with you. Charles Foster Kane is a scoundrel; his paper should be run out of town; a committee should be formed to boycott him. You may, if you can form such a committee, put me down for a contribution of one thousand dollars…."

(*Now serious, bending over the imaginary Thatcher who is in the chair*)
"On the other hand, I am the publisher of The Inquirer. As such it is my duty – and I'll let you in on a little secret, it is also my pleasure – to see to it that decent, hard-working people of this community are not robbed blind by a pack of money-mad pirates, just because they haven't anybody to look after their interests! …I'll let you in on another little secret, Mister Thatcher – I think I'm the man to do it. You see, I have money and property. If I don't look after the interests of the underprivileged, maybe somebody else will – maybe somebody without any money or property – and that would be too bad…."

"You're right, Mr.Thatcher. I did lose a million dollars last year. I expect to lose a million dollars this year. I expect to lose a million dollars next year. You know, Mister Thatcher – at the rate of a million dollars a year – I'll have to close this place in… sixty years."

Kane can afford to run with the foxes and hunt with the hounds.
If he's a radical at all, he's not the pious kind (for they're the truly dangerous ones).
No, Kane has no belief in the possibility of a perfect world,
nor even a near-perfect world. He's not a social engineer.
He's not an engineer of human souls.
He's covering all the angles for *himself*. The only thing he really cares about is *him*.

"In Xanadu did Kubla Khan
a stately pleasure dome decree;
where Alph, the sacred river, ran
through caverns, measureless to man,
down to a sunless sea.
So twice five miles of fertile ground
with walls and towers were girdled round...
It was a miracle of rare device,
A sunny pleasure dome with caves of ice."

So you see, Coleridge gives it to us on a plate.
Kane's ice-palace has to be Xanadu.
Nothing can stop Kane as he becomes the Ghengis Khan of publishing!
As time goes on, he fills his palaces with the loot of the world - and captive
wives - but takes no joy in any one of them, except the act of ownership.
At length, forlorn, he wanders through a maze of labyrinthine halls,
great drawing rooms and imposing staircases the size of amphitheatres.
The living world, its shafts of warmth and light, can barely penetrate
the cold vastness of this dark place – a mausoleum of emptiness!

Rosebud

And as for 'Rosebud', do we ever really know?
The first, fine, careless rapture of a child?
A toboggan, and the thrill of sledding on the snowy slopes of innocence?
In the movie it's committed to the flames.
Only Kane perceives what 'Rosebud' means for him.
Only you know what it means for you.
We each wear Rosebud in our heart's lapel.
It's rosebuds, rosebuds, all the way;
the Mona Lisa's smile, the Sphinx's stare,
the passing of a girl with flaxen hair.
Maybe that's the romance of the rose?

"O Rose, thou art sick.
The invisible worm
that flies in the night
In the howling storm
has found out thy bud of crimson joy
And his dark secret love
Does thy life destroy."

(Change of tone)
On the other hand, consider this. Rosebud's just – a clitoris!
And not any old clitoris either! We got it from someone (can't remember who)
that this was Hearst's pet name
for the favourite aspect of his girl-friend's personality.
That was a pretty shitty thing to do. But we did it. And Hearst knew.
The old man had always striven to protect
the privacy of Marion Davies. It obsessed him.

The War of the Worlds furore had been an accident.
But with Kane we knew what we were doing.
We <u>wanted </u>to provoke a public sensation!

I'm just about to have revealed the golden rule that teaches us
'Never pick a fight with someone more ruthless than yourself.'
The night we launch in San Francisco, I'm alone in an elevator when
the gates crash open and in walks – Hearst.
Then they clatter shut. Just him and me. And silence
that speaks stridently of wrath to come.
With all the jauntiness I can muster (well, he was buddies with my father),
I ask him 'Would you like two tickets for the show?'
He fixes me with those steely blue eyes,
and with the calmness of an executioner selects a button
for the thirteenth floor. It seems to take a lifetime (and it does).
And then, with tranquil rage, he walks right past me.
I call after him: "I really don't know what the trouble is, old man,
Charles Foster Kane would have accepted them."

Hearst's reply is less well known and it was this:
'Mr Welles! You think you have destroyed me…
what you don't realise yet is that you've destroyed yourself.'

The drama of my life has reached its 'point of no return',
as I am threatened with a lawsuit of quite terrifying beauty.
His mighty empire blacks me out. And he slaps a boycott on me! Worse!
He tries to get the film withdrawn as 'communistic',
because his labour union enemies just love it.
Ergo, Welles must be a communist! No cinemas or movie-chains will book it.
(Fox-West do buy, but only to ensure it won't be shown.)

But all this is as nothing to the 'noises off'!
Hearst's personal Gestapo have files on every Hollywood executive.
He's threatening to 'expose' them all as rapists, alcoholics
and 'miscegenators', whatever that's supposed to mean.
His highly-placed lieutenants spread the word
that the proportion of Jews in the industry
has, so far, gone un-noticed, but that it might not be possible
to conceal such 'information' from the public for much longer!
Already, some Jewish heads of studio are running scared.
They offer eight hundred and five thousand dollars
to buy the masters and get 'Kane' burned alive.
The tactics pioneered by Doctor Goebbels were paying off!.

I want to put it on in tents, marquees all over and bill it as
'The show they don't want you to see!' I want to buy the film myself
(it would have meant financial security for life),
but RKO and Schaefer won't agree.

And yet Kane is only partly based on Hearst. I'd met a few such men
among my father's business circle, sort of prematurely embalmed in gold;
like Tut-en- Khamen, spiritually imprisoned by the liberty that wealth bestows;
confined and stunted by infinity of choice. Great Gatsby's of our time,
believers in … 'the green light, the orgiastic future, that, year by year,
recedes before us. So we beat on, boats against the current, borne back ceaselessly
into the past.'

Sometimes I imagine old, successful Kane trying to retrace his steps back towards the younger Kane, striding forth towards his destiny - and the thought occurs …that their two paths may never, ever meet. They're like two people who have not been introduced.

I'm beginning to realise just what I'm up against, sitting in a restaurant some place, when a friendly detective sidles up to me and says 'Don't go back to your hotel room tonight! They have a fourteen-year-old, naked girl in your closet and two photographers.'

As I walk the streets awhile, I feel my every step is being watched. I feel….terribly…alone. And I have no idea what's in store for me…

(Anton Karas zither chord. The lights begin to dim down. Then with controlled anger, he shouts)

No.No.No! …Cut!…What the hell are you doing, Lou! Don't dim the lights on me!…There's nothing in the script says we fade out at this point! Godammit! It's not the end of the story, is it? Don't answer that! Maybe some people think it is, but they are wrong!

Optional End of Act One
I n t e r v a l

ACT TWO

The Empire Strikes Back

'For every act of creativity, there is a punishment.'
Just when everything is going for you –
that's when you should start to know …
it's all behind you and it's downhill all the way from here on in.
When everybody wants to shake you by the hand,
is the moment when the wise man sees the shadow of
the knife above his shoulder,
poised to cut him down to size; transform the noble savage
into a dancing bear, shuffling in his shackles
for charitable pennies, thrown in pity.

But to pin-point that defining moment when the Prince becomes
apprentice to the role of clown, amidst the din of accolades,
the plaudits and the songs of praise is not so easy.
Success breeds envy and galvanises
the collective wrath and guile of all my adversaries.

They wait a while to choose their moment and
when it comes, it's not the frontal assault you might expect.
Oh no, far greater subtlety than that!
I'm on the second picture of my contract.
It's called 'The Magnificent Ambersons', which I produce, direct, narrate,
For which I also write the screenplay.
It's going to out-Kane Kane. A mid-west family saga,
much like the one I'd known, and based upon a novel by
Booth Tarkington (another buddy of my father's).
It's all about the illusion of progress,
and how time gnaws ceaselessly away at greatness.
It's in the can. It's done and dusted but for the editing.
I am well into this process, when Nelson Rockefeller
takes a hand in things. At this time, the arch-Republican
is serving Roosevelt's administration at the State Department.

He takes time out to inform me
That it's my patriotic duty to spend a million dollars.
And that, alone, should have struck a warning note!

' Mister Welles? Good of you to make time to see me.
 Now, Orson – I hope you don't mind me
using first name terms? - Good. Good…and you can call me 'Nelson'.
Well; Orson, I have a proposition to put to you, which might be to
our mutual advantage…It would mean you get to help your country
in its hour of need…Yes, I thought that might appeal to you…The President is
looking to roll back Nazi influence in South America… We need a kind of
…Special Ambassador and, well, we thought you might be just the man!
Of course, I'm serious. We've given it a lot of thought…Your movie contract?
Don't worry about that! Why, you could make a movie set around the Rio
Carnival.
Yes – two birds, one stone. We really need a quick decision…You'll do it. Great.
I knew I could rely on you. I'll tell the President. You know, he's a
great fan of yours.'

(Welles walks downstage a little)
Rockefeller and Schaefer guarantee that I will have the right to make the final
cut
for Ambersons. It's an offer I can't refuse.

Beware of kings bearing three gifts!
You see, Rockefeller is also on the board of RKO,
a sizeable holding, and Kane's upset his influential friends
as well as doing nothing for the value of his shares.
And so, I'm stranded in the jungle, like Lucifer expelled from Paradise,
thinking things are going well - when Schaefer's ousted
and a butcher's knife is given to Charles Koerner
to carve out the magnificence from the 'Ambersons'.
This was the unkindest cut of all, the fulcrum of my life.
You may sense the paranoia of conspiracy here.
But why dump miles of my footage at the bottom of the Pacific? Why?
I say an enemy hath done this!

Unless perhaps it's something even more mysterious?
Stranded in the darkness of the rainforest,
I'm about to shoot a voodoo dance… when the witch doctor
demands payment for his dancers' new costumes.
My budget's gone. I'm broke. There's nothing left.
The priest is furious and puts a curse on me.
That night, I find a knife piercing through the script
I'm working on - 'It's All True!'
Attached to it is …a ribbon of red wool!
Nothing will be the same from this day on.

My Radical Credentials

I know of a memorandum, filed by one J.Edgar Hoover. It's marked 'for the
attention of the Attorney General of the United States'.
You may find it amusing, now. It wasn't funny at the time.
Here's how it read:
"For your information, the Dies Committee has collected data
indicating that Orson Welles is associated with the following organisations,
which are said to be of a communist nature – The Negro Cultural Committee,
The Medical Bureau and North American Committee to Aid Spanish Democracy,
The Motion Picture Arts Committee, The Workers' Bookshop,
The American Student Union,' etcetera, etcetera. The list is long.
But I could add a lot of other suspicious activities to this list –
the kind of truly crazy things you do in the heady days of youth!

Like leading the drive to sell war bonds for the government;
doing radio talk shows for the US Treasury;
campaigning with Roosevelt in Boston;
and broadcasting for the Democratic Party national committee.
Why! They even want me as Vice-President!
But come on! Me? A divorced movie actor at the White House!
I don't think so!
One thing I do regret though. The President is keen I
stand for Senator in Wisconsin and I turn him down.

The Republican candidate is a guy called…Joseph McCarthy.
I might have saved us all a whole heap of trouble,
had I taken him on, but I chickened out, the numbers didn't add up.
As for J.Edgar Hoover! You should see *my* files on *him*!
But why should you be interested in his wardrobe?
Or his taste in off-the-shoulder ball-gowns?
Still, just because he's a transvestite,
doesn't make him a communist now, does it?

(Opening rising clarinet cadence of Gershwin's 'Rhapsody in Blue'
and first few bars. Fade…)

Lovely Rita

Returning from the jungles of Brazil, by way of Mexico,
my senses hotly tuned to the exotic, a restlessness
within cries out for serious attention.
Some overpowering energy, the motion of a gathering wave
that lifts you bodily within its glassy swell
to wash you on a wild fantastic shore;
delirious, in awe, of all creation's marvels.
It is a picture in a magazine called, simply… 'Life'.
And on its cover, is a woman with a mass of flowing
hair, as red as molten lava, cooling as they touch
bare arcs of silken shoulders as it nestles there.
Her form is long and languorous, sheathed in black,
the sleekest panther in the prowling trees of night.
Dream-mistress of an army, gored in Armageddon's war.
Her smiling eyes betray a vulnerable child,
within the provocation of the pose. Her parted lips
demurely whisper pure incitement, 'Ravish me!'

*(Subdued background noise of poolside party chatter and
the clinking of ice in cocktails)*
I start to tell the world that I and Rita Hayworth will be wed,
(Rita doesn't know it yet.) Joe Cotton throws a party for me
and I head off to meet her there, like a killer bee
in search of some bee-eating Venus-trap.
Rita's there. *'I've heard about your wedding plans'* she says.
    - 'Is there a problem?' I reply.
'Yes, Victor wouldn't like it. We're engaged, you know'
    - 'Oh, Victor. Nice guy! But a little… immature, for you, I think.
He's the only actor I know with bigger tits than his leading ladies!'
She whispers back *'I like my beefsteak, rare,'*
-      'Well they don't come any rarer than me.'
'Yes, you just got in from Mars. Tell me, how's the weather there?'
- 'Oh, sultry. And the women, mostly green, look all the same to me.'

Married by September nineteen forty three,
(they call us 'Beauty and the Brain')
we have a child, Rebecca, nineteen forty four;
and separate in forty-five. In forty six, she tries to reconcile,
but it kind of spoils things when I bring my latest flame on set
as Rita plays 'The Lady from Shanghai.'
None of it is Rita's fault, of course. She loves me but
she only feels secure when we are close.
- I mean …as close as you can get!
As for me - I just can't leave the dames alone…
Marilyn…and Judy Garland are consuming all my energies.
The revenge of lovely Rita is deserved, and truly awful.
She starts a thing with Howard Hughes.
They rendez-vous for assignations in a beach-house
owned by Marion Davies, of all people!
Now is that poetic justice or what!

As the Lady from Shanghai, Rita was magnificent –
a dark secret at the centre of a maze of intrigue.
She's both the victim and the source of all the
brooding evil that ensnares the scheming men,
who are attracted to her like filings to a magnet.
I cut off her hair and dye it blonde.
And, when the film is shot, I split with her…
That's the fate of all my women.
They may *think* they have the leading role, but
it's all a celluloid illusion. I'm the star.

The Third Man

You never really know when a movie part's going
to take off for you. The most unlikely roles can suddenly
become a moment in screen history, even if you're not the star.
It's the late forties. The cold war has just frozen over the Danube,
and I am cajoled by Carol Reed into taking on this part.
(To be frank, I need the dough to shoot my movie of Othello)
…Anyhow, I guess I'm on screen no more
than ten minutes – most of those, long shots
in the sewers of Vienna – bad for my lungs!

I play a low-life mobster selling black-market penicillin
which cripples sick children and kills only the lucky ones.
It's hardly an heroic part but it puts the hero, Holly Martins,
in the shade. He doesn't get the girl. Lime does!

(Slow fade to near darkness over the next nine lines)
Just what is it about Harry Lime that makes her mourn for him?
Why do audiences thrill when they first discover
Lime's not dead, after all? Why do they half-hope he can
escape his honourable pursuers and cheat death, yet again?
The author, Graham Greene, knew what it was.
The Devil is a charmer. His songs are sweeter.
He holds a sinister fascination for all mankind.

His persuasiveness is legendary.
Lime and Holly Martins have just reached
the topmost point of the ferris wheel at a fairground.
It's a long way down!

(Performance piece. Blue spot, Swelling sound of Anton Karas playing the 'Harry Lime Theme')

*Look down there. Would you really feel any pity
if one of those...dots stopped moving forever?
If I said you could have twenty thousand pounds for every dot that stopped,
would you really, old man, tell me to keep my money?
Or would you calculate how many dots you could afford to spare?
Free of income tax, old man. Free of income tax,
the only way you can save money nowadays....
When you make up your mind, send me a message.
I'll meet you any place, any time and when we do meet, old man,
It's you I want to see...not the police. Remember that, won't you?*

(He starts to walk away. Returns to spot)
*And don't be so gloomy.
After all, it's not that awful. You know what the fellow said:
In Italy for thirty years under the Borgias they had
warfare, terror, murder, bloodshed – They produced
Michaelangelo, Leonardo da Vinci and the Renaissance.
In Switzerland they had brotherly love.
They had five hundred years of democracy and peace,
and what did that produce? The cuckoo clock! So long, Holly..."*

(End of performance piece. Wash lighting.)

Those last few lines were mine. I just wish to God I'd written the rest of it!
Yes, dear old Harry Lime, sold his soul to the devil !
Well, no one dare accuse me of <u>that!</u>
I picked a fight with Lucifer quite early on.

As a career move, it wasn't very smart,
for, sure as hell, the devil runs the show.
I have to beg and plead to get the dough
to start each movie, then scrimp and save to
bring it to the screen. It's no way to live your life.

Commercials

These days my movies are financed by frozen peas.
And people sometimes ask do I lose sleep
each time I do commercials, just for cash?
(You must have seen me selling steaks, fish fingers, frozen veg?)
I have to tell you now it never bothers me one jot!
Why, all my life I've been selling Peter to pay Paul!
I've done it from my earliest years. It's the only moral thing to do
if you really want to make the movies you believe in.

Why is it no-one ever stops to question the morality of those
who deal in movie-crap, ten million bucks a throw?
'Blockbusters!' – I'm just not into busting blocks.
Never have been. Strictly for the cons!
No thanks! I like to keep reality in focus:
the sin of avarice, the corrosion of the soul by power;
how things turn into dust the moment you possess them
and are possessed *by* them;
how youth is sick with age and innocent corruption;
old men despised in wisdom, and …woman, whom,
no matter what the manner of her falling,
is never quite deserted by… divinity.

These things obsess me. Yet I suppose I am
no better or worse than my contemporaries.
As a legendary scorpion once said to his trusting friend the frog –
'I can't help it. It's my nature'

OK so that's *my* personal commercial to you. Now let's talk about the real ones.
Have you any idea of what goes on behind the scenes
in making a commercial for…the humble garden pea? Y'know?
-those little green things you scrape to the side of your plate
when all the steak has gone? They're superstars and they get to have
an inflated sense of their own self-importance. I know of garden peas
taking home a salary you could feed a whole family on for a year,
while movie makers, like me, intone in reverential requiems, the voice-overs–
careful never to upstage the tiny vegetables!
Don't get me wrong here. I'm not prejudiced.
Some of my best friends are small and green.
But the peas I'm speaking of have villas in Bel-Air,
with swimming pools and their own private mint-gardens.
They trash hotel rooms while on tour and their private lives
are split open like pods and chewed over by gossip columnists.
In thirty seconds flat you can witness
… 'The Tale of Two Peas',
their rise to fame, how they are introduced by a mutual friend,
a honey bee, and know the minute their eyes meet that 'this time it's for real!'
They grow tall on their beanstalks, mature and then
are cut down, frozen, packed and jet-set to your dinner table.
I give my best in doing justice to this tragedy – but there's a limit!
And one day, I reach it…

(The italic lines are spoken by Welles as a director of the commercial)

We know a remote farm in Lincolnshire where Mrs. Buckley lives.
In July, these bare snow-covered fields burst into pea blossom…

Cut! Mister Welles can we do another take on that one, please?

Why? I thought I hit just the right tone there.

Again please Mister Welles. And this time could you stress the 'in'. You know,
the line …'In July, these bare snow-covered fields…'

Why? That doesn't make any sense. Sorry. Stress the 'in'?
You're asking me to stress the preposition that precedes the noun?
Perhaps I should stress **into,** too. That would truly screw it up. Or better still…
In July **these** bare snow-covered fields burst **into** pea **blossom.**
Now it's totally subverted. What do you say? Shall we do it?

Please Mister Welles. Were not writing a grammatical primer here…

Come on fellas, you're losing your heads.
I wouldn't direct any living actor like this in Shakespeare.
If I emphasise the 'in', the balance and the metre of the line is compromised.
That's just idiotic, if you'll forgive me saying so. That's just stupid.
Surely even you can see, in the depths of your ignorance,
the rhythm of the piece breaks down entirely.

Mr Welles, again please? It's not 'Othello'…

You're damn right it's not Othello. It isn't even William fucking McGonagall!
(There's a long silence while they eliminate McGonagall from their enquiries.
And I'm getting madder by the minute) '**In** July'? You're serious?

*Yes please, Mr.Welles **In** July these bare snow covered fields….OK ! Let's go!*

No! It's not OK! It's impossible. Meaningless.
(To himself) It isn't worth it. No money is worth it!
(To director) If you can demonstrate to me how
I can speak these lines by stressing prepositions whilst still
retaining metric discipline, why I will pledge myself to
personally go down on you and much may you enjoy it.
It'll be something to tell your grandchildren **in** the future!
Now did you get **that** on tape! Release it to the press!

(He starts to dress for the part of Falstaff)

I guess I was a little harsh on him.
It's frustration, I suppose ….because every commercial I do
slowly chips away my image as an actor.
A spectacular amusement and a massive insult to the hungry!
A fat man advertising how to put on still more weight!
(It's enough to make consumers turn consumptive!)
Have you seen me lately? Why! I'm almost three hundred pounds!
I can fill a panoramic screen in long-shot!

That Tun of a Man

So…here I am, a raggle-taggle gypsio, exiled to the foyers
of hotels in London, Paris, Rome, Madrid,
and living off the land. The lean years have begun,
and they get leaner as my girth expands.
I drink and eat my way through continents.
I swim a channel of the finest clarets, sherries, chardonnays.
It started in Vienna, where I'd be glued to cake-shop windows,
like a little boy in an Aladdin's cave of calories!

Schwartzeveldetorte…Gugelhoopf…Borgeteaterlinse…
Topfenschnitten…Kafecremetorte…Nustorte…
Ebercreme…Italienische gemischte…Cognac frichte…
Streissel…Kerfelguger…und Zagertorte..

Each day, before me, in the glass, I see the outward image
of the man I have become…

(with increasing disgust)

"There is a devil haunts me in the likeness of an old fat man -
that tun of a man, that trunk of humours,
that bolting hutch of beastliness, that swollen parcel of dropsies,
that huge bombard of sack, that stuffed cloak-bag of guts,
that roasted Manningtree Ox with the pudding in his belly,
that reverend vice, that gray iniquity, that father ruffian,
that vanity in years…Wherein is he worthy…but in…nothing?"

(He throws a cloak around himself with a flourish)

I have to throw a cloak around my girth to cover it.
It also cloaks…my disappointment with life, around this time.
One night, on TV, I come across the ruins of the 'Ambersons' again.
The sadness of it gets to me… and I break down in tears.

Becoming Falstaff

Is there any magic left? Can I turn adversity to my advantage?
I've grown into the part I love the most. Sir John Falstaff
needs no support from pillows, stuffing, padded jerkins!
I can now play him in the raw! He's naturally gross by virtue of his appetite for
life. 'You are what you eat' the anorexics tell us.
Falstaff is what Falstaff eats – mutton, beef and venison, sherry, sac and ale!
He's eating for the world – because he *is* the world.

(Sits in the chair.)

We have heard the Chimes at Midnight. Do they ring a bell?
The ageing prankster, fat with self-indulgence, exiled from the court of pageantry,
where the fates of men are fashioned. Do they strike a chord?

He's hardly Don Quixote and he doesn't have the tragedy of Lear.
And yet, there's something poignant, something deeply personal, here.
No longer can he over-ride the stern realities of power
by the mere force of his imagination and preposterous wit.
I feel that Shakespeare's writing of a man, who, in his heart,
still lives in Merrie England; that golden time when the hay smelled sweeter,
where the village and the countryside, it's conjured tales and legends
prevailed above the machinations of the modern world.
Falstaff is irreverent, an enemy of pomp, a chocolate soldier.
He has no time time for 'honour', 'bravery' and 'courtly protocol'.
He despises them. He only wants that he should live to tell the tales
of battles where he triumphed in his own absence.

Falstaff is totally ungovernable. To use a modern phrase 'He's out of it!'
Maybe Hamlet stayed in England and grew fat?
(Some of us *are* like that, you know). It says a lot for the English
that, of all the mighty characters the Bard creates, this… faker is
the most adored by groundlings, the most anticipated, rapturously received,
the most lamented in his passing
and the most welcomed in his resurrection.

" I would your Grace would take me with you; who means your Grace?…
That he is old, the more the pity. His white hairs do witness it.
But that he is – saving your reverence – a whoremaster – that, I utterly deny.
If sac and sugar be a fault, God help the Wicked!
If to be old and merry be a sin, then many an old host that I know is damned.
If to be fat is to be hated, then Pharaoh's lean kine are to be loved.
No my good Lord; banish Peto, banish Bardolph, banish Pointz,
But for sweet Jack Falstaff, kind Jack Falstaff, true Jack Falstaff,
valiant Jack Falstaff, and therefore, more valiant, being, as he is,
old Jack Falstaff, banish not him thy Harry's company –
banish plump Jack and banish all the world! "

"I do! I will!"

The Nose I never got to play.

I'm a great believer in noses.
It could be said that noses got me into acting in the first place.
I was led by the nose and led a few others into the bargain.
I was on holiday in Ireland, just sixteen, and landing up in Dublin.
T'was a fine summer!
I breeze confidently into the Gate theatre, where, with a combination
of blarney and baloney, I manage to convince directors Hilton Edwards
and his partner Micheal Mac Liammoir that my juvenile excursions
into theatre at Todd School for boys constitutes something
of an established acting career. They're a charming couple.
Whether they fall for my yarn or not, I'll never know.
(He pulls out a box of noses)
But after a brief audition, they go along with the wheeze.
And it's now I need every nose I can lay my hands on
to cover up my baby face and play the parts of characters
twice, three times my age. I figure I get through every nose
in the props-room in a few short months.
So, I start my own production line in noses.

A nose every play keeps the critics at bay!
Never use the same nose twice, and, if possible,
change noses in the second act. It's true in movies, too.
If you've got a cute little nose like mine, get it written
out of the contract and demand a separate dressing room
for your new, bigger nose. A big nose ensures you'll
be taken seriously. Every actors trailer should have one.

But there's one nose I never got to play: Cyrano de Bergerac.
To help a friend, he is contracted
to write love poems to a beautiful lady, the object of his friend's desire.
The poems of Cyrano win the lady's heart,
but she cannot find the poet in
the man she marries. The two do not add up.

She learns, too late, the true identity
of her great love – a poet with a monstrous nose,
whose soul is just as grand and generous.
In a tranquil grove, they finally meet;
two pure hearts, united for eternity
by all their years of separation and denial.

I tell you, when they play that scene – it's Kleenex time!
A time for the blowing of noses. Only a Frenchman could have written it!

F for Fake

Et maintenant…Messieurs-Dames! Je vous voulez,
ecoutez a l'histoire d'un magicien for-mi-dable!
I'm spending so much time in Europe these days,
they've adopted me. And, do you know – I figure
some of that old 'sophistication' and 'complexity' is finally rubbing off.
I think my mother would be proud of me.
I've stumbled on a story so subtly convoluted,
so replete with ironies within enigmas, that it will blow the minds
of all those calculating sceptics back in California.
At last I can confront the shallow world of Hollywood
with some penetrating intellectual insights.

It's the seventies and the French are having a high old time
-'deconstructing' everything that moves.
Barthes, Foucault, Jacques Derrida triumphantly declare
'The Death of Authorship!' And this is very odd, because
the books that carry this obituary have the author's names clearly
printed on the cover and earn them handsome royalties.
How's that for sophistication!
The French are really rather good at such duplicity.
I have my own doubts, though, since, back home,
some shallow mistress of the borrowed word
declares Orson Welles never wrote a word of 'Citizen Kane'!
Well here's one author who will not die!

To those who trade in backstage vanities and speculation,
I recommend a trip to Chartres, where they should stand a while,
as it has stood for centuries – a cathedral to God's glory
and the dignity of man. His premier work - and it's without signature!
You know it might be just this one anonymous glory, of all things;
this rich stone forest, this epic chant, this gaiety,
this grand choiring shout of affirmation, which we choose
when our cities are dust, to stand intact;
to mark where we have been and testify to what
we had within us to accomplish

The works of man are spared for a Millennium or two,
then wear away to ultimate and universal ash;
the triumphs and the frauds, the treasures and the fakes
confront this fact of life – that all of us are going to die!
Maybe a man's name doesn't matter all that much.

The Waiter's Tale

There's a story doing the rounds which may or may not be true,
depending on who's re-telling it and what construction
the listener puts upon it.
Take one. It's around 1980.
I walk into an empty restaurant and survey the menu disinterestedly.
The only waiter on the premises approaches me and enthuses,
quite innocently *"Ah! Mister Welles!...I loved your movie!"*
"Which movie?" I reply.
"The one about the newspaper guy... Kane...
Tell me...have you made anything since?"
I sigh a wry smile, order fettucini, eat and leave without a word.
Take two. A tale told by a waiter. It's around 1980.
I walk into a *busy* restaurant and *ogle* the menu *hungrily*.
I am approached by a waiter. *"Ah! Mister Welles...I loved your movie!"*
"Which movie?" I reply.
"The one about the newspaper guy... Kane..
Tell me...have you made anything since?"

I throw down the menu in disgust.

" Have I made anything since? "(***Breaking into a rising tirade)***

How's about (***reels them off ever faster)***

The Magnificent Ambersons, The Stranger, The Lady from Shanghai, Macbeth, Othello, Mr. Arkadin, A Touch of Evil, The Trial, Chimes at Midnight, The Immortal Story, F for Fake…and finally, let me ask *you* a question, why don't you stick your fuckin' fetuccini up your ass!?

The crowded dining room is stunned to an embarrassed silence.

I slam the mirrored door behind me and it shatters.

Take one was the reality. But if you prefer, take two. <u>You</u> be the editor.

<u>You</u> decide!

(***Still raging, he picks up film cans and starts throwing them down)***

And then there are …all these. The films I <u>didn't – couldn't -</u> finish!

It's All True! Don Quixote, The Deep, The Other Side of the Wind!

And dozens more!

(***Finally, trying to bring his anger under control)***

Life, my friends, is <u>not</u> a movie script. If only!

It's just a bunch of out-takes from the cutting room floor,

from movies you <u>imagined</u> you were making.

I've got cans of them stacked up in my own private Xanadu.

Maybe some day, someone will come along

and stitch them all together. Maybe <u>that's the story,</u>

and the secret's in the editing! ! A ribbon of dreams!

Have you ever thought…that, at the heart of all this creativity

lies frailty? You could even call it folly.

God is safely in his coffin, while movie-makers deify themselves,

as Roman Emperors once sought the mantle of divinity.

'They told me I was everything. Tis a lie! I am not ague proof!'

Today, instead of crowns, we wear the cap and bells, like clowns,

cavorting in the dust of an expendable universe.

(He stands. Blue square of light. The last performance piece)

'*Delight is to him, who, against the proud Gods and commodores of this earth stands forth his own inimitable self. Who destroys all sin, though he pluck it out from under the robes of Senators and judges! And eternal delight shall be his, who, coming to lay him down can say "Oh father, mortal or immortal, here I die.*
I've striven to be thine, more than to be this world's or mine own.
Yet this is nothing. I leave eternity to thee – for what is man,
if he should live out the lifetime of his God?"'

Cut! (*House lights up. Casually but upbeat.*) OK Lou! Let's wind it up, right there!
(Strolls around, dons fedora) Same time tomorrow! …Maybe, to finish, I'll just come down stage and do my usual…
(He comes downstage with a flourish of fedora)
'Ladies and Gentlemen, I remain, as always, ..your obedient servant!'
(As he does so, he pulls a white rabbit from his trousers, tosses it aside and strolls off, hands in pockets. Harry Lime theme)

THE END

"Rosebud: The Lives of Orson Welles" is a project born out of the remarkable prior, and continuing, international success of a previous collaboration between partners Mark Jenkins, the author, and Josh Richards, the director.

The book is available from
www.infestedwaters.co.uk
and leading bookstores